Original Poems
By Earl J.
"Nickey" Picard

Cypress Cove Publishing

PRAISE FOR Nickey Picard's Book

I have always had great fondness and respect for the outstanding public service of Earl J. "Nickey" Picard as Lafayette's City Marshal for over 30 years and his decades of law enforcement even before that. But this collection of his poems has shown a soulful, thoughtful and observant side of Nickey as well. From the most deeply felt poems about his beloved "Angel," his wife of over 70 years, to musings on friends, colleagues, and even traffic safety and politics, Nickey Picard has proven himself a prolific and keen observer of the human condition. I am amazed at how prolific Nickey's writing is - so personal and heartfelt about his private and public lives. But especially about his beloved Jeanette. Well done, Nickey, I'm so proud to know you.

Carol Ross, local radio talk show personality

Having grown up on the Northside of Lafayette and witnessing the Picard Family in law enforcement, fire protection and on the golf course, it was a pleasure for me to read Mr. Picard's poetry book. From "I Did Not Know" to "Why Lafayette Is Greatest," the short poems illustrate Nickey's life through his daily experiences. His journey is well documented, and the book is the compilation of many years in a community that has changed in so many ways.

Gerald Boudreaux, Louisiana State Senator, District 24

I have known Earl "Nickey" Picard most of my adult life. I first met him in the 1960s when he was assisting the Lafayette Parish District Attorney in a criminal case that I was defending. I have known him to be exceptionally successful in everything that he has undertaken, especially as Lafayette City Marshal. I have told people that I thought that Nickey was one of the best politicians that I have known. I also know him to be a man of God, with a love for his family and his country. One thing that I did not know about him until recently is his love of poetry. I have read his Book of Poems and was "blown away" with the quality and content of his work. I am not a great connoisseur of poetry, but this is good stuff. It is easy reading and helps tell a story of a man and his life. I will recommend this to everyone as worthy of purchasing and reading.

Earl Taylor, Former District Attorney, St. Landry Parish, Louisiana

The Staff and Attorneys of our law firm were collectively blown away by the compelling, articulate, creative and inspiring poetry of Earl "Nickey" Picard in his new book of poetry. While most of us have followed Nickey and his poetic pursuits for decades, and all of us have been duly impressed by his talent, none of us expected the type of insightful, invigorating and unique pieces of work that are the insignia of this work.

With all my heart and soul, I would recommend a thorough review of this book of poems by anyone who cares about great artistry, communication and deep-seated inspiration. Nickey's poetic ramblings are the literary stuff of life, contentment and love.

Glenn Armentor, President and General Partner - The Glenn Armentor Law Corporation, Lafayette, Louisiana

Mr. Nickey Picard has a passion for poetry, and it has been great to follow his work. I am thankful for his friendship and his sharing his second love, his poetry.

K.P. Gibson, Sheriff, Acadia Parish

In this unique collection of poems, Louisiana Author Nickey Picard tells in poetic verse true stories of the past with its sorrow, war and death, and the present with its sweet success, anger and fear of the future.

Connie Gremillion, author of *A House for Eliza*, and *Never Say Goodbye*

Mr. Picard is a man of many hats and talents. He is loved by many and respected by all. Each poem captures the event of that day, a memory of the past, his concerns for our future, love for his community and fellow man, his faith, and his Cajun Heritage. Nickey shares more in his poem, 'I am Proud to be a Cajun.'

Pictures included in this book add interesting details of what was on his mind or why the poem was written. He seems to be able to let the words flow and shares his heart and thoughts in poetry form. His poems are full of history, dates and important issues of everyday life shared from his heart. He is a great storyteller. Thank you Nickey for publishing your poems for others to enjoy.

Sudie Landry, President, Writers' Guild of Acadiana, Lafayette, LA

This Book is Dedicated to my Dear Wife

Cecille Jeanette Dupuis Picard

Born 1933 - Died 2019

Published by:
Cypress Cove Publishing
PO Box 91195
Lafayette, LA 70509-1195

Hardcover ISBN-13: 978-1-936707-37-9
Softcover ISBN-13: 978-1-936707-38-6

Library of Congress Control Number: 2020912158

- Edited by Neal Bertrand
- Interior design by Jeremy Bertrand, Cypress Cove Publishing

Other Titles Published by Cypress Cove Publishing

Down-Home Cajun Cooking Favorites; 6x9 paperback, $14.95
Rice Cooker Meals: Fast Home Cooking; $14.95
Slow Cooker Meals: Easy Home Cooking; $14.95
Cajun Country Fun Coloring and Activity Book; $4.95
Fun Times Puzzle and Activity Book; $9.95
Fun Times with Math-Logic Puzzles; $9.95
Fun Times Cajun Puzzle & Activity book; $9.95
A House for Eliza: The Real Story of the Cajuns; $15.95
Never Say Goodbye: Real Stories of the Cajuns; $14.95
From Cradle to Grave: Journey of the Louisiana Orphan
    Train Riders; 8x11 hardcover, $26.95
Dad's War Photos: Adventures in the South Pacific; $19.95.
Louisiana Legacy: History of the Daigle and Schexnayder
    Families; by Edward Daigle; 6x9 paperback, $19.95
Grow Up Into Him: Bible Word Studies to Live in Victory;
    8.5x11 paperback, $19.95

The Spiritual Warfare Series by Sudie Landry
◊ Silent Prayer: A Spiritual Journey Toward Exposing the
   Occult – Level One; $14.95
◊ Trail of Six Roses: Supernatural Events at Mother's
   Funeral - Level Two; $6.95
◊ Mom Bradley's Crossover: From Deathbed to Heaven –
   Level Three; $8.95
◊ Supernatural Encounters of the Godly Kind – Level Four;
   $14.95
◊ Prayer Warrior: The Life of a Seer – Level Five; $14.95

Visit CypressCovePublishing.com for all of our latest
books.
To order, see our website,
or call Toll Free (888) 606-3257,
or buy from Amazon.com.

Table of Contents

About my wife.

I DID NOT KNOW

I did not know my heart could hurt so much
Not until I could no longer feel your touch
I did not know I could cry a million tears
Not until I lost you after all those years
I knew my arms would miss you so
They never wanted to let me go
I knew my lips would miss
They're ever longing for your kiss
I know I've cried a million tears
Since I've lost you after all those years
Now I know my heart can hurt so much
Since I no longer feel your touch
It only took a little while
For me to miss your loving smile
I love and miss you so
So much no one will ever know

I wrote this on the night my Angel died,
November 19, 2019.

ALL NIGHT I SAT AT HER BEDSIDE

All night I sat at her bedside
Prayed and prayed, and yes I cried
My Angel was not doing well
She was really going through hell
Tried her best to get some sleep
Perhaps her pain was much too deep
I held her hand, kissed her cheek
She tried to smile but it was bleak
All happiness had left her face
And misery just took its place
Her silver hair was not in place
No longer had that radiant face
Yes we have the ugly answer
Her lungs are ravaged, by Stage 4 CANCER

On our 70th Wedding Anniversary we renewed our vows. At the celebration with friends and family I read this to my wife.

THREE SCORE AND TEN YEARS TODAY

Three score and ten years today, we both said "I Do"
Two young kids in early teens,
God knew our love was true
Some did say this would not last
Because they thought it was too fast
We knew that they were wrong
We knew our love was strong
We just knew our love would grow
We loved each other so
The years went by, and here we are
"LOOK AT US", proud we came this far
We have one girl and two big boys
They all made their share of noise
We were young and yet mature
We had a love that would endure
I watch her sleep, I smile and pray
all through some joyful tears
I pray for God to let me hold her,
for more happy years
She is my friend, she is my wife
But most of all, she is my life
We will always hold those memories dear
THANK YOU ALL FOR BEING HERE!

I wrote this one night after my wife died, and began sleeping in our bed again.

I SLEPT WITH YOUR PICTURE LAST NIGHT

I slept with your picture last night
It was placed on your pillow, a beautiful sight
It was like the good times when I held you near
With your face so radiant and smile so clear
I spoke to you about all our years
All those great times without the tears
It was peaceful and quite late in the night
You were right there with me, holding me tight
My love for you only grows and grows
How much I love you, God only knows
You will forever live in my heart
Nothing will cause us to be apart
You were my Angel here on this earth
You became my wife fifteen years after your birth
I know you are in Heaven with our loving God
Your love for me has made me proud

I wrote this on the first Mother's Day since my wife
passed away.

THIS BASKET FULL OF ROSES

This basket full of roses, I got these just for you
I love and miss you baby with my love so true
Many years or the sting of death,
will never change my love
You are my Angel watching over me
from Heaven up above
I've cried at least a million tears,
my eyes are never dry
Just the mention of your name and I begin to cry
The pain I feel is always there, it never goes away
For I miss and love you so, I just cry and pray
I miss you more as each day goes by
Just the mention of your name and I begin to cry

This is about my first Christmas without my wife.

THIS WILL BE MY FIRST CHRISTMAS WITHOUT YOU

This will be my first Christmas without you
I don't know what to do
I love and miss you so much
I miss your soft and loving touch
Through tears I keep looking for you
I don't know what to do
Your sweet smile I will not see
It was always you and me
I have never been without you
I don't know what to do
Over seventy years of love with you
I don't know what to do
We held hands to sleep
Never had to count on sheep
Life was fun, our love was true
I don't know what to do
One thing I will surely do
I WILL KEEP ON LOVING YOU!

70 YEARS, 7 MONTHS AND 16 DAYS

For 70 years, 7 months and 16 days,
God sent you to me
For that period of time in my life,
I was happy as I could be
Our love did flourish, our lives were full
There was no fighting, no shove nor pull
Love and happiness were easy to find
For we had love and peace of mind
Every day was a day filled with love
I loved you and you loved me, and God above
We were young, but we both knew
The love we had was real and true
We loved our girl, and our two boys
They all did make their share of noise
God then called you, my Angel home
Since you're gone there's been much gloom
But I thank God for all those years
Filled with love and without tears
I know someday we'll meet once more
And there will be more love galore

EVERY DAY GETS TOUGHER

Every night gets longer
Every minute missing you gets stronger
You are on my mind at every turn
My flame for you will always burn
Our house you left is full of you
My love for you, is oh so true
Not a day goes by that I don't cry
And turn to God and ask Him why
I visit you at your place of rest
Going back home at not my best
I get back home you are not there
Face to face with this nightmare
Every day gets tougher, every night gets longer
Every minute missing you gets stronger
Not a day goes by that I don't cry
And turn to God and ask Him why

I wrote this to my late wife.

OH HOW I LOVE YOU

Oh how I love you, oh how I miss you
My love has always been so true
The many years I had you with me were great
My love for you were years of love not fate
I could not love you anymore, I gave you all I had
Only the time I lost you, I hated really bad
Losing you did change me, not my love for you
At times I look to heaven I don't know what to do
I sense that you are near me, how I wish you'd be
Yes when we were so happy you at home with me
Our house is not a home to me it's just this place
Where I go to look for you, and your lovely face
I know one day we'll meet again in a happy place
Where parting and sadness have no displace

This is one of several poems I wrote and presented at the 100 Club Banquet held each year at the Petroleum Club where local Police Officers were recognized and honored for work above and beyond their call of duty.

A BADGE

A badge is a symbol, of trust we can't abuse
It is a source of power, we never should misuse
We must not dishonor, ourselves for other men
We harm all those around us, when we choose to sin
We must never tarnish such a noble shield
No matter what we're offered
we can't succumb and yield
We must never weaken, and join the other side
We can't give in to money, nor let it be our guide

A badge is a symbol, which must be worn with pride
It must remain unsullied, with not a thing to hide
We must not be tempted to use it in a way
Which would harm others, by what we do or say
The oath that we all took, is one we cannot break
Those words we must remember,
for there is much at stake
A badge is a symbol, of trust we can't abuse
It is a source of power, we never should misuse

I wrote this of how I feel when I see our great flag.

EVERY TIME I SEE
OUR COUNTRY'S FLAG

Every time I see our country's flag,
a sense of pride just fills my chest
Every time I see our country's flag,
I'm reminded that we have the best
The reds are true, the whites are pure
All colors bright to long endure
Fifty stars in a field of blue
Set in there for me and you
A gift from God blessed by His hands
We have the best of all the lands
Every time you see our flag,
a sense of pride should fill your chest
Every time you see our flag,
recall that God gave us the best

Photo by Jp Valery on Unsplash

1974 was a bad year for the flu nationwide. People were calling in sick almost every day and describing their ailments to supervisors and employers. It was a bad year.

A PATHETIC POETIC SICK CALL

I'm calling you
I've got the flu
My head feels light
My chest is tight
My throat is dry
My fever high
And when I sneeze
I do by threes
As for my cough
No better off
I hack and hack
But it won't crack

My body aches
I get the shakes
I feel a drip
Upon my lip
I blow my nose
The mucus flows
But now it's clogged
And I feel flogged
My ears are plugged
I'm really bugged
It hurts to grin
I won't be in

I wrote this poem while in the State Police in 1956. In 1954, Ford introduced safety belts, safety door locks, and collapsible steering wheels and other so-called safety devices which were touted in other makes of cars. 1954 was one of the better years and President Dwight D. Eisenhower announced a National Auto Safety Program, and 1955 was going to be a very safe year. 1955 turned out to be the worse year in the history of highway safety, as we killed and injured more people in 1955 than any year in the history of highway safety. The reason for this is that drivers were given a false sense of security and safety. What was needed was defensive driver education courses.

A NATIONAL DISGRACE

It has been termed a "national disgrace"
The manner in which the human race
Kills and cripples on our roads each year
Leaving an ugly and bloody smear
By speeding, drinking and reckless driving
The whole year long we keep depriving
Men, women and children of life so dear
Leaving millions of others in constant fear

Our roads are the sites of ugly scenes
Broken bloody bodies and torn machines
People dying and suffering in terrible pain
These scenes are seen again and again
There are little children bloody and hurt
Pinned in the wreckage covered with dirt
Their poor little bodies take a terrible jar
When some were thrown away from the car

Should we continue this mass "blood spilling"
Should we continue this needless killing
Continue to drink, continue to speed
The rights of others should we fail to heed
We will make this year the same as the last
Taking no notice to what we've done in the past
And by so doing another time
Our disgrace then, will be a **"national crime"**

Two good friends of mine got married in Lafayette, and I was invited to attend the marriage ceremony. I wrote this poem and sent it to them as a congratulatory note.

DANA AND GLEN

Dana and Glen were married tonight
On the banks of the river, what a beautiful sight
Their garden was filled and those in the crowd
Were friends and relations,
with the blessings from God
They spoke their vows truly, all present could see
This most blessed union, was just meant to be
Their love for each other,
just grew through the years
Seeded with laughter and watered by tears
While on their new journey, God looks from above
As they travel this road and strengthen their love
God surely will bless them and pray to ensure
Their love for each other, will ever endure

This is one of the several poems I wrote for the
Police Memorial Program held in May of each year
with the Lafayette Police Department.

DEAR GOD, GIVE US THE WISDOM

Dear God, give us the wisdom,
to guide us as we serve
And pray we give the people,
protection they deserve
Keep us ever mindful, we chose to serve mankind
And we must never falter, nor ever be unkind
Laws like your commandments, in your famous book
We must always honor, as the oath that we all took

Dear God, give us the wisdom, we need to overcome
The threats that we encounter,
brought about by some
Keep us ever mindful, of those who thrive on greed
They will stop at nothing, to hatch their evil deed
For laws and your commandments,
they will not abide
But from your final judgment,
they have no place to hide

And as we honor heroes,
they served and gave their all
They carried out their duties, on their final call
Keep us ever mindful, of those who paid the price
They served with fearless courage,
never thinking twice
Dear God, give us the wisdom,
to guide us as we serve
And pray we give the people,
protection they deserve

In 2005 I was honored to be inducted in the Louisiana Justice Hall of Fame. Each inductee was given time to make an acceptance speech. Colonel Grevenberg was the first person to pin a badge on me when I joined State Police and General Stroud had been my Commanding General in the National Guard. They were inducted at the same ceremony. I made mention of the General and Colonel in this poem.

AS I ACCEPT THIS HONOR

What this honor means to me, I truly must confess
The pride and awe I'm feeling now,
words cannot express
This was not achieved alone,
one man is not that great
There were those behind the scenes,
in me they kept their faith
As I accept this honor, it's not just for me
But for all those people, helping this to be
I pray and thank my God, for His granting me
The chance to serve mankind,
and get to knowing thee
My good wife and children, they believed in me
Despite those times life was hard, on our family
I thank my Mom and Dad,
they taught me wrong from right
They put me on a path, which led me here tonight
I must thank my siblings, they too played their part
Most of them are gone today, still always in my heart
Those with whom I serve, their loyalty sincere
They gave that extra push, to help me make it here
I wish to thank the General, and the Colonel too

Both of whom were models,
who helped me make it through
The badges that I've worn, I always wore with pride
And pray each day not to misuse,
the weapon on my side
I learned respect is earned, it must be given first
It cannot be demanded,
from one you have just cursed
Grateful for this honor, you have my word tonight
I'll not disgrace this honor,
I pledge to do what's right
I thank you for this honor, and not just from me
But from all those people, helping this to be

I wrote this about how our President Trump was being treated.

DEMOCRATS AND RINOS

How can they hate, one man so much
They must be really out of touch
So out of touch, so filled with hate
At every turn, they doom their fate
The people see, the people hear
Every day their end comes near
We see their circus on our TV
This is not how things should be
No respect for oaths they took
Raised right hand, one on "THE BOOK"
Felons stand to testify, even if it is a lie
Their agendas clear, they blink no eye
How can they hate DONALD TRUMP so much
They must be really out of touch
They are the ones who will be affected
They guarantee he will be re-elected!

I wrote this poem in 1953 when I was a Trooper and investigated an accident caused by a drunk driver. This was one of my first of many and I wrote it on my way to the hospital, morgue and my Troop Headquarters afterwards. I was given a Certificate of Recognition by the Director of Safety and the poem was printed and distributed by an insurance company with my permission at no charge.

DID YOU?

Did you ever see an accident?
Where bodies as well as steel were bent
Mangled, twisted and torn apart
Because some joker thought he was smart
Did you see him standing by the side of the road?
Trying to hide his "heavy load"
With bloodshot eyes and messed up hair
His clothes disorderly and he did not care
With a smell of liquor upon his breath
And a smile on his lips as though laughing at death
Staggering, near falling, when trying to walk
Not understood when trying to talk

Did you look at the others lying there still?
So mangled and twisted it made your blood chill
Did you say to yourself, "what a terrible shame"
And looked at the "joker" placing the blame
Well friend I don't blame you, not one little bit
For in the chair of a murderer this "joker" could sit
As he turned his car into a weapon of death
And pulled on the trigger as this car he met
But unlike the murderer it was not intended
Though he could not prevent the way it ended
For like all "drunken drivers" he could do no good
As liquor controlled the power under the hood

I served as Marshal for 30 years and 7 months in Lafayette. In my attempt to educate the public on just what the Marshal does I wrote this poem and put in on the back of my business card, especially as it pertains to drunk drivers once they were booked, charged and released on bond.

DRUNKEN DRIVERS
GET OUT ON BOND

Drunken drivers get out on bond
It is my job that they be found
They must be served to be in court
The date and time they must report
That is my job and if not done
They get away and they have won
Rest assured they will not win
I'll do my job and get them in
Warrants are issued by the court
For those of them who don't report
They may run but they can't hide
"Father Time" is on my side

I am a member of the Kiwanis Club of Lafayette and their major fundraiser is the Kiwanis Football Jamboree. I would purchase an ad in the program and I wrote this poem and put it in the program as my ad. I also put this in the Lafayette Advertiser as well.

FOOTBALL FEVER

Football fever is in the air, kickoff time is here
One can hear the marching bands,
hear the people cheer
Those touchdown runs and field goal tries,
will be alive and well
Broken plays and passes dropped
will leave some tales to tell
Hearts will pound and some will scream,
as the games go on
As "first and ten, do it again,"
come from a megaphone

Those young men, who play the game,
will give their very best
And hope the fans will all agree,
that they have passed the test
Win or lose they give their all, it's all that they can do
It means so much to all of them,
to get support from you
To all the teams the best of luck,
throughout this football year
Go injury free and have clean fun,
so all of us can cheer

This is one of several poems I wrote for the Police Memorial Program held in May of each year with the Lafayette Police Department.

FOR EVERYONE WHO WEARS A BADGE

For everyone who wears a badge,
we gather here to pray
That God goes out, with each of them,
as they work their way
We pray that all, will be kept safe,
as they patrol their beats
As they work hard, and hours long,
making safer streets
We pray that God, will give them strength
to serve for public good
And pray that all the work they do,
may be understood
For in these days, and at this time,
support is what they need
To halt the scourge, of crime and drugs,
and the growing greed

We gather here and pray for those,
who were taken from our ranks
And as we pray for each of them,
we express our thanks
The sacrifice that each has made,
was made for you and I
And you and I, should not forget,
what they did and why
We must go on, because of them,
and carry on each day

For what we do, we do with them,
while with God they pray
That you and I, be safe and sound,
as we patrol our beats
While we work hard, and hours long,
making safer streets

State Trooper badge awarded to
Earl J. "Nickey" Picard upon graduation from the
Louisiana State Police Academy, June 1953

This is one of several poems I wrote for the Police Memorial Program held in May of each year with the Lafayette Police Department.

GOD GIVE US THE COURAGE

God give us the courage to turn back the tide
Brought about by evil men who will not abide
They no longer have respect, they will not conform
All they bring is misery, all they leave is harm
No, they don't know you God, for they are the thugs
Everyday they ruin more lives
with their deadly drugs
Young and old fall victim to these vicious men
They have no guilty feelings for they live in sin
God grant us the courage to turn back this tide
Pray we stop these evil men who will not abide

Those of us who wear the badge,
form a thin blue line
We must keep these evil men,
yes from yours and mine
God give us some comfort as we come to pray
Heroes made the sacrifice, we honor them today
Yes, they are our heroes, we must not forget
What they gave for all of us, so we would never fret
We pray too for loved ones, ones they left behind
We pray for God to bless them,
give them peace of mind
God, we ask Your blessings, as we join to pray
We sadly miss our heroes and honor them today

This is one of several poems I wrote and presented at the 100 Club Banquet held each year at the Petroleum Club where local Police Officers were recognized and honored for work above and beyond their call of duty.

GOD BE MY "BACK-UP PARTNER"

Dear God, don't let me tarnish,
this shiny badge I wear
Don't let me be a villain, don't let me be unfair
Keep my weapon holstered,
and pray that I won't need
Such force that could be deadly,
or termed a foul deed
Don't let me use this power, to crush my fellow man
Let me show compassion, in cases where I can
Make me ever mindful, of people and their plights
And pray I always honor, basic human rights

Should my life be threatened,
by those who won't conform
Be my "back-up partner", protecting me from harm
Pray with me for loved ones, who worry about me
Give us hope and courage,
to serve mankind and Thee
As we pray for comrades, who died for you and I
In honor of their memory,
help keep our standards high
Dear God don't let us tarnish,
these badges that we wear
Don't let us be the villains, don't let us be unfair

This is one of several poems I wrote for the Police Memorial Program held in May of each year with the Lafayette Police Department.

GOD LOVES ALL POLICEMEN

God loves all policemen, this I do believe
Regardless of their title or patch upon their sleeve
City, state or parish they are all the same
And when they serve the people,
they do it in His name
He is out there with them every day and night
He's there with every movement,
yes He keeps them in sight

God loves all policemen and we should love Him too
For when you need His comfort,
He will be there for you
When you need His guidance He will not be far
You will have to do no searching,
for He's the brightest star
God loves all policemen, give your love to Him
You will know his goodness,
your hopes will never dim

God loves all policemen and as we pray tonight
For those who've gone before us,
I'm sure they're in His sight
They are up there with him standing by His side
And praying for our safety, in God we can confide
God loves all policemen, this we can believe
Regardless of their title or patch upon their sleeve

On July 23, 2015 there was an active shooter at the Grand Theatre 14 here in Lafayette. I wrote this poem the night of this tragedy and placed it on my Facebook page.

GRAND TRAGEDY

He calmly walked into the Grand
Filled with hate and gun at hand
He shot and shot not one he knew
Wounding nine and killing two
How can a man just be that cold
To randomly shoot the young and old
How much hate must one possess
To hurt or kill and caring less
For all the grief his acts will bring
There is no excuse for such a thing
He killed himself he could not run
In his attempt he turned his gun
Though this act will haunt us long
Lafayette will come back strong
For we will pray and thank our Lord
And as we do, keep up our guard

These two deputy city Marshals in Marksville,
Louisiana were indicted by a grand jury on
December 10, 2015 on charges of 2nd Degree
Murder and attempted 2nd Degree Murder in the
killing and wounding of a 6-year-old autistic boy and
his father on November 3, 2015.

GREENHOUSE AND STAFFORD

Greenhouse and Stafford, a killing pair
Killing young Jeremy, a child so fair
He had no chance against their hate
He was so young for such a fate
They shot his dad and shot him too
They had no defense from this rotten two
Behind a badge they hatched their deed
For life and limb, they had no heed
This little child, just barely six
Had no defense for dirty tricks

Now the court must do its job
To eradicate this "wannabe mob"
Put them away where they can't kill
No more innocent blood should they spill
What a stain on the human race
With this cruel and evil case
God will judge them in the end
The rules of life He will not bend
They will pay for what they've done
To this dad and his young son

This is another poem I wrote about the drunk driver.
I put it on my Facebook page in an effort to attempt
to prevent drinking and driving.

HE KNOWS NOT WHAT HE WILL DO

He knows not what he will do, as he leaves that bar
He is drunk and at the wheel, of a two-ton car
He will leave the parking lot, taking to the street
He cares not what he might do, sitting in that seat
As he drives, he thinks he's fine,
even though he's not
He has had more than a few, he has had a lot
He may weave, may even speed, no one really knows
He is drunk and at the wheel,
down the street he goes
Should he chance to run a light, thinking it is green
What about that other car, coming on the scene?

Why do those who choose to drink,
get behind the wheel
Do they think they can control, that two tons of steel
Can't they see this can't be done, many tried and lost
Don't they see the price is high, oh the human cost
How can one not truly know,
gas can't mix with booze
Don't they know, have they not heard,
"DRINK AND DRIVE YOU LOSE"
If you drink you should not drive, plain as it can be
We must stop, its up to us, squarely you and me
If we don't, then shame on us,
we can't blame the booze
We know now for we have seen,
drink and drive you choose!

I was inducted into the Living Legends Acadian Museum in Erath, La on September 26, 2009 and I wrote this as my acceptance speech.

I'M PROUD TO BE A CAJUN

When God created people, He did from A to Z
And when He got to Cajuns,
I'm glad that He made me
I'm proud to be a Cajun, from a Cajun mom and dad
To give me Cajun parents, He blessed me as a lad
God gave me something precious,
when He gave me life
Then He really topped it off, I got a Cajun wife

I've lived in Cajun country,
since the moment of my birth
This is the only place I'd choose,
to live upon this earth
I've been to many places, and know I'll never find
A better place I'd rather live,
which gives me peace of mind
We know it's true that Cajuns,
have hearts of purest gold
Our love and care for people,
is there for young and old

God took a piece of heaven, and put it in our state
Then He made the Cajuns, to make it really great
Yes, God in all His wisdom,
just knew when it was done
When He made the Cajuns,
they would be number one
When God created people, he did from A to Z
And when he got to Cajuns,
I'm blessed that he made me

I wrote this poem to use with groups when I spoke about our great country and what we stood for.

I'M PROUD TO BE AN AMERICAN

I am an American and very proud
I say this proudly and say it loud
This is my country, I love it so
I want the whole wide world to know
Born and reared in this great land
To keep it safe I'd gladly stand
I know that God gave us a hand
In making this the greatest land
Many came from lands afar
To live the dream or catch a star
Every time our flag I see
I truly feel it's telling me
"Come here my son, I'll keep you free
My stars and stripes and field of blue
Will always fly and wave for you
Many died to keep you free
Almighty God meant this to be"
Every time our flag I see
I proudly feel it waves at me

I was the First Sergeant of the 256th Combat Engineer Company, Louisiana National Guard at Opelousas and was nominated by my Commander as "Senior Non-Commissioned Officer" in 1982. The convention was being held in Bossier City and I was to appear to be boarded by a group of regular Army Command Sergeant's Major. On my way there with my wife, I wrote this poem on a napkin while I drove in the event I would be selected. I appeared before the Board and interviewed and the next day was announced as the winner. I read the poem as my acceptance speech. The poem was later printed by the Guard and distributed.

I AM PROUD TO BE A GUARDSMAN

I am proud to be a guardsman,
prepared to do my share
To help my friends and neighbors,
though hardships they may bear

I am proud to be a guardsman,
and proud to serve my state
There is so much satisfaction,
the feeling's really great

I am proud to be a guardsman,
yes proud that I can be
Part of an organization that keeps this country free

I am proud to be a guardsman,
and for the chance to show
My trust in this great country, and how I love it so

I am proud to be a guardsman,
for all these things are true
I feel that it's a privilege, to serve with folks like you

I am proud to be a guardsman, I will always try
To serve the guard with honor,
and keep my head held high

I am proud to be a guardsman,
and know we're not alone
For there are many others,
to come when we have gone

I am proud to be a guardsman, and I feel pretty sure
That God, the Greatest Guardsman,
will help us to endure

Awarded for Senior Non-Commissioned Officer
of Louisiana, in 1982

As a kid I would see the Vegetable Man
almost every day.

I KNEW THE VEGETABLE MAN

I knew the Vegetable Man, in my childhood days
I knew him as Mister Leo,
and miss his friendly ways
He was a business man, selling his crop each day
With his horse and wagon, he would make his way
With his loaded wagon, he went from street to street
Always with a respectful and pleasant greet
The people would wait to flag him down
For his produce was the best in town
I saw the "Vegetable Man" as a husband and dad
Who gave to his family all the love he had
Times were hard and sometimes bitter
ONE THING SURE HE WAS NEVER A QUITTER!

On November 3, 2015 this 6-year-old autistic child
was a passenger in a vehicle driven by his father in
Marksville, Louisiana when they were stopped by
two deputy city marshals. The two deputy marshals
fire 18 rounds from their weapons into the vehicle,
striking the father twice and striking the young boy
five times, fatality wounding him.

JEREMY

This innocent child was savagely killed
His innocent blood was shamefully spilled
He had no defense from gun toting thugs
Caught up in crimes and possibly drugs
Wearing a badge under color of law
Behavior so cruel and manners so raw

Having no chance, they shot up his dad
He was unarmed, no chance had he had
No way could he try to save his child
From these two thugs who had gone wild
They have been charged and held in a jail
They are both held there waiting on bail

In all of my years, I have not seen
None so cruel, nor none so mean
Yes, they will have their day in court
The date and time they must report
A jury trial they both will face
To defend themselves from this disgrace

In time they'll face "The Man" upstairs
This is the Judge who truly cares
He will ask "What have you done"
"You shot a man and killed his son"
"They had no chance; you had no right"
"Now you must pay for wrongs that night"

I was invited to a veteran's memorial service for
Memorial Day and I wrote this poem and presented
it at that function.

MEMORIALS ARE REMINDERS

Memorials are reminders, reminders of the past
They help us to remember
and make the good thoughts last
Remember every soldier who gave their lives so we
Would never lose our freedom
or country strong and free
We gather here and we pray
that God will show the way
To live in peace and not destroy
the life we have today
Memorials are reminders of freedom and of peace
And a plea to God above that every war will cease

Memorials are reminders and those who serve today
Must also be remembered as we stand here and pray
For they stand tall and ready to defend this land
From those with greed and evil,
yes, we must take our stand
We must take a stand today,
a stand that we will keep
This great country safe and sound
and nights with peaceful sleep
Memorials are reminders of freedom and of peace
As we make this plea to God
that every war will cease

I wrote this about one of my dreams.

MY DREAM LAST NIGHT

My dream last night was clear and cool
God was back in every school
As we prayed "Our Father's Prayer"
I felt His presence everywhere
I sensed the gladness and the cheer
I saw the smiles from ear to ear
It was no longer against a rule
For the Lamb to be at school
How I wish this dream were true
I pray to God you wish it too

Mr. Clarence Thibodeaux was a longtime law enforcement officer in Lafayette Parish. In the late 1940s he served as Chief of Police in Scott, Louisiana. He later served with the Lafayette Parish Sheriff's Department where I met him while I was with State Police. He later served as Chief Deputy City Marshal for Marshal Dallas Broussard, Marshal Donald J. Breaux and as my Chief Deputy when I was Marshal. Since that time his granddaughter is presently married to my youngest son, who served as my Chief Deputy after Mr. Thib retired.

MR. THIB

Mr. Thib, we love this man,
we know what he has done
A very kind and gentle man, a friend to everyone
In his way he brought to us, yes, every single day
His little jokes that only he,
knew when and how to say
This good man was always there
and always last to leave
He never took vacation days and this you can believe
Mr. Thib did his job well, and he looked out for me
But he looked out for all the guys,
and this was plain to see
This fine man gave of his time,
to help all those he could
And even those he could not help,
they surely understood

In the years that I have known
this good and honest man
He always tried, as he would say, "I'll do it if I can"
Mr. Thib, a family man, yes, full of love and care

A working man, a thoughtful man,
yes, he was always there
This gentle man made many friends,
has them by the score
I don't know of anyone, who might have even more
Now today as he retires, we hope he stays in touch
Yes, all of us wish him the best,
because we love him much
Mr. Thib, I'm sure you know,
our prayers go out to you
So you enjoy the years to come,
in all the things you do

This poem is about my late brother who died in
1989. He was probably one of the best amateur
golfers in Louisiana. I nominated him for the
Louisiana Sports Hall of Fame. This poem was
intended to be read at his induction if selected. He
was not inducted.

MY BROTHER
AND THE GAME OF GOLF

My brother loved the game of golf,
and he played it well
And I believe the game loved him,
this I sure could tell
This love affair was started young, with a piece of tin,
He quickly learned to swing a club, and began to win
A club and ball, both made of tin,
hole dug in the ground
He played the game with such desire,
like a Master's round
We later got a regular club, and a regular ball
And I saw then that he would play,
with the best of all

With fork and spoon we'd weed the greens, earned
green fees this way
Out on the Course we caddied on,
we would get to play
With blistered hands, our backs still sore,
one club to our name
We could not wait to hit the ball,
for we loved the game
We caddied then and we did learn,
watching others play

50

And Shirley was, yes we all knew,
that he'd be good someday
He bested most at early age, winning was his style
He played his game, and he could drive,
yes a country mile

The "Moose is Loose," one headline read,
from a friend no less
Some called him "Moose" for he was strong,
but he had finesse
The pitching wedge he mastered well,
as he went his way
Yes, playing rounds and setting marks,
which still stand today
A fifty-eight for eighteen holes, thirteen under par
Yes he could putt and pitch it well,
not just drive it far
He won the state and many crowns,
I can't name them all
He truly was a gifted man, with golf club and ball

A Cajun boy who mastered golf, care he did not lack
He never did forget his roots,
he gave something back
Though very ill, he still went out,
yes, to teach the game
To boys and girls, not doing this, for any fee or fame
Yes Shirley loved the game of golf,
and he played it well
And I believe the game does miss,
this guy who gave it hell
While I believe that it was meant,
for him to play the game
I do believe that he should be,
placed in the Hall of Fame

I wrote this poem for a traffic safety program and used it in annual safety programs at Thanksgiving when I was a member of Louisiana State Police in the 1950s.

MY THANKSGIVING PRAYER

I thank Thee Lord for what Thou hast done,
within the passing year
I thank Thee Lord for not being one,
who has killed a child so dear
The strength and power Thou hast given me,
to drive my car with care
Has steered me from some foolish acts,
and others from despair
I thank Thee Lord for granting me,
the wisdom needed to foresee
The foolish acts of others
that could have killed or injured me

Oh Lord I give Thee thanks today,
for all that Thou hast done
And pray that in the years to come,
that each and everyone
Will drive their car always with care,
and give consideration
To all the people on the roads,
in this great united nation
Oh Lord I pray that Thou wouldst grant,
your children this one plea
I thank Thee Lord this Thanksgiving Day,
as I send my prayers to Thee

I wrote this on my 86th birthday.

NO SMOKE, NO MIRRORS, NO MAGIC TRICKS

No smoke, no mirrors, no magic tricks
Tomorrow turning eighty-six
And now I have this little grin
Yes, if I could, I'd do it again
It's hard for me to realize
These many years have passed my eyes
Some were "blah," but most were fun
And I remember every one
Forty-three were young and forty-three were old
Those in between, BEST BE LEFT UNTOLD
Now Medicare and Retirement Pay,
I never thought I'd see this day
No smoke, no mirrors, no magic tricks
STILL HERE THANK GOD…FOR EIGHTY-SIX!

On 9/11/2011 I was seated in the waiting room at a doctor's office that morning. The TV was on, there was video but no audio, and I saw the planes hitting the towers. Then I noticed the trailers on the bottom of the scene and went to the TV and turned the volume on. It was then I got the awful news about what was going on. I wrote this poem the week before the first anniversary in 2002 and read it at the event on 9/11/2002.

NINE ONE-ONE, TWO THOUSAND ONE

Nine one-one, two thousand one,
our lives did change that day
When men from hell came from the skies,
and took our peace away
Our televisions carried, the horror and the grief
Millions watched the carnage, in total disbelief
Thousands died as buildings fell,
crashing to the ground
And as we speak this very night,
some have not been found
Just ordinary people, on an ordinary day
Going about their business, in an ordinary way
Many safety personnel, rushed to render aid
While many so responded, with their lives they paid
Some were wearing uniforms, police and firemen too
They were out there doing the jobs they swore to do
No one could imagine, those horrors could be real
As many cameras focused, on all that twisted steel
Our country was the target,
of men so filled with hate
They killed just to get numbers,
knowing well their fate

Our strength was not diminished,
our resolve is strong
We brought it to those devils,
who chose to do us wrong
They provoked a peaceful giant,
who has searched them out
In no uncertain terms they know,
yes what we are about
Those who died will be revenged,
and peace we will return
For peace throughout the whole wide world,
is now our main concern
Nine one-one, two thousand one,
our lives did change that day
Now them who sent those men from hell,
they have a price to pay
God will bless America, this great land of the free
"One Nation Under God," we are and we will be

I wrote this poem to use in Drug Abuse Prevention Programs that I was conducting.

"NO"

Just say "NO" and mean what you say
Should a pusher of drugs approach you someday
This two-letter word will tell him you don't
Your message he'll get and bug you he won't
Just say "NO" and be on your way
Just ignore his sales pitch, or what he may say
Don't fall for his lies, just tell him to split
But mean what you say, I'm sure he will quit

Just say "NO," but make a report
This will be the first step to get him in court
Yes, give the police his name if you know
For when this is done, they'll get him in tow
Just say "NO" and trust in the law
Report what you heard, relate what you saw
When we show these rats we really mean "NO!"
Streets will be safer, wherever we go

There was talk about removing the phrase "One Nation Under God" from the "Pledge of Allegiance." I wrote this poem as my opposition to such a move and a growing disrespect for our country and flag.

"ONE NATION UNDER GOD"

"One nation under God," what an awesome phrase
Every time we say it, we give our country praise
There are some who question,
why we think this way
Some have even told us, there is no need to pray
How can some believe this,
how can they say it's wrong
And question words we use, in a patriotic song
Prayer is not permitted, where children go to learn
"Old Glory" isn't safe,
from those who choose to burn
Just who they think created,
this world in which we live
Who they say we're hurting,
by thanks we choose to give

This is the greatest country, there is no better place
We care and we are thoughtful, of every single race
We clothe and feed the hungry and we aid the ill
To those we've liberated, we never sent a bill
We help the whole world over, help in times of grief
We never turn our backs, on those who need relief
While we know that freedom, really isn't free
We will defend the freedom, of those who want to be
"One nation under God," is an awesome phrase
We should be proud to say it,
give God and country praise

Back in the 1950s Louisiana law required all vehicles
to stop at railroad crossings to make sure the tracks
were cleared before proceeding across.
People were cited by State Police for failing to stop at
railroad crossings.

RAILROAD CROSSINGS

Railroad crossings everywhere
Need to be approached with care
Railroad signs are placed out there
But you and I must drive with care
Crossing gates and signals too
Are designed for me and you
So we will know and must adhere
Signals mean a train is near

Rainy days and foggy nights
Make it hard to see the lights
Other signs are there to warn
Like ringing bells and blowing horn
We have to look and once we hear
Warnings that a train is near
We must stop and we must wait
For the lifting of the gate

We must never try to race
Any train at any place
This is such a foolish game
This will kill and this will maim
This is why we cannot chance
We must do more than take a glance
Railroad crossings everywhere
Need to be approached with care

I wrote this poem back in the late sixties or early seventies to use in drug prevention programs. It was printed in our local Kiwanis Club newsletter that I was a member of in Lafayette.
The word spread about this poem and it was printed in the newsletter of a Kiwanis Club in Australia.

RECIPE FOR DRUG ADDICTION

First you start by sniffing glue
Then you pop a pill or two
Next you light a little pot
Now you mix the stuff you've got
Add to this some LSD
Halfway through the recipe
Keep this up a month or two
Mixing with a little brew

Now you add the morphine pill
Hype it for a quicker thrill
Next the heroin you mix
This provides the bigger kicks
Now you've had it, it works well
Makes your life a living hell
Face this truth, it's not fiction
This recipe for drug addiction

The Sunday when I visited Grace.

SEVERAL SUNDAYS BACK

Several Sundays back I went to a wonderful place
One blessed by God, they call it Grace
I was a stranger there but not for long
I made new friends during their first song
One man hugged me saying, "They call me George"
He wasn't big but his faith was large
He was the Pastor of this great place
I quickly saw why they named it Grace
He led prayer and his love of God
His voice was strong and he was proud
The choir sang songs and they were great
You could sense their love and feel their faith
What I saw and heard in this great place
I will always cherish that time at GRACE!

He came to us in eighty-three.

"SULLI"
(Honorable Michael G. Sullivan)

He came to us in eighty-three
He was our first Division "B"
A nicer man will not be found
He was a joy to be around
He loved to laugh, a "regular Joe"
A better man we'll never know
He was a man of style and grace
The type of man you can't replace

He ran his court both firm and fair
He was a Judge with "People Care"
You always felt at ease with him
He would not act on just a whim
You always knew just where he stood
He did his job and did it good
Yes "Sulli" was among the best
This gentle man is now at Rest

This is one of several poems I wrote and presented
at the 100 Club Banquet held each year at the
Petroleum Club. Local police officers were
recognized and honored for work above and beyond
their call of duty.

TARNISHED BADGES

Our badges have been tarnished, by actions of a few
They've brought about suspicion
of everything we do
They've placed us under microscope
and now a probing eye
Is watching every single move, made by you and I
They've hurt the very people,
that they swore to serve
I'm glad our justice system,
metes out what they deserve
They've harmed a proud profession,
insulted me and you
Our badges bear the tarnish, of actions by a few

We need to keep on working, to do the best we can
To carry out our duty, to serve our fellow-man
Most have served with honor, integrity and pride
Most are like an open book, with not a thing to hide
Let us not give reason, let us not give cause
Let us leave no questions, as we enforce the laws
We will remove this tarnish, we will clear the dust
We will convince the people,
that we deserve their trust

This is another poem I wrote about the drunk driver.
I put it on my Facebook page in an effort to attempt
to prevent drinking and driving.

THAT "DRUNKEN DRIVER"

That "drunken driver," he's done it again
Ruining a life and causing more pain
He uses no gun, nor uses a knife
His car is his weapon, for ruining a life
He gets himself loaded, then takes to the road
While weaving or speeding, unleashes the load
His victims are people, who haven't a clue
Of such foul deed, he surely will do
He gives them no warning, gives them no chance
No way to know what he'll do in advance
He strikes them so quickly, no time to react
From out of the blue, a crushing impact

Men, women and children, are murdered this way
"I only had two," is what he will say
He'll go into court, to plead in his case
All suited up, with a smirk on his face
He'll try to suppress, he'll try to delay
And hopes they forget, it may go away
He'll make some excuse, he'll follow a plan
He'll lie to the court, he'll do what he can
He'll make them believe he's seen a new light
And given a chance, he'll do what is right
But that "drunken driver," he'll do it again
Ruining a life and causing more pain

I was a member of the Louisiana National Guard and during a recruiting drive I wrote this poem and the Commanding General chose to reprint this poem to be used during the recruiting drive.

THE GUARD

The Guard provides a way to learn
A way to lead, a way to earn
A check each month is at your door
A way to earn yet even more
A way to meet and make new friends
All while your rank and pay ascends
A way to earn retirement pay
No cost to you and "that ain't hay"
Tuition paid for college too
A part-time job that's good to you

We need good folks to fill the ranks
To man the guns and drive the tanks
To climb the poles and string the lines
Build the bridges and lay the mines
To draw the maps, to type and file
To tend the ill, bring back a smile
Drive the trucks and fix them too
Prepare the "chow," for those who do
The Guard belongs, won't you belong
And help to keep our country strong

I wrote this about wearing the Marshal's Badge.

THE MARSHAL'S BADGE

For thirty years and seven months,
the Marshal's Badge I wore
For thirty years and seven months,
I maintained an open door
For thirty years and seven months,
I lived the oath I took
Each day I did my job, it was like an open book
For thirty years and seven months,
I worked and trained each day
For thirty years and seven months,
I sought a better way
For thirty years and seven months,
no scandal did take place
For thirty years and seven months,
not the slightest trace
These thirty years and seven months,
will always be with me
"VERY PROUD, I WAS IN THAT CHAIR TO SEE"

The Honorable Kaliste J. Saloom, Jr. was Lafayette
City Judge from 1953 to 1993, the longest serving
judge in Lafayette City Court history.

THE JUDGE

For forty years he sat the bench, since 1953
He was the only sitting judge, til 1993
Many folks, who broke the law,
would shudder at his name
But to this court, and to our town,
he brought reward and fame
For those who chose, to drink and drive,
he really did get tough
And to support, the traffic laws,
he could not do enough
He started schools and programs too,
for those who broke the law
He did his best, to do his job, without a single flaw.

Throughout the years, he sat the bench,
he always gave his best
He set a pace, there was no slack,
he always stood the test
The cases moved, no undue wait,
he granted few delays
And when he did, he made it known,
the time was within days
He sat the bench, into the night, if this is what it took
And as he ruled, on every case, he did it by the book
They recognized him, many times,
for work that he had done
Yes, he is why, this city court,
was rated number one.

Now forty years, have come and gone,
and he has earned a rest
And we are gathered here today,
to wish him all the best
We wish him well, when he pursues,
that golf ball on the links
To drive it straight and drive it long,
and all his putts he sinks
We wish him, the best of health,
the best that life can give
He made our town, a better place,
a safer place to live
For forty years, he sat this bench,
whoever takes his place
Might fill the job, but not his shoes,
his steps they can't retrace

I wrote this poem after investigating a major
accident near Abbeville where five young men were
traveling to Abbeville. Their vehicle, apparently
traveling at a high rate of speed, left the roadway and
entered a ditch and hit a culvert, killing twin
brothers, one being the driver and two of their
friends seated in the back seat with a cousin of theirs
who survived the accident with very serious injuries.
This was in 1956 when I was
with the Louisiana State Police.

THE KID BEHIND THE WHEEL

How many of you when driving,
upon the roads today
Meet the kid behind the wheel,
going along your way
How many of you have blamed him,
for the reckless way he drives
And say he is responsible
for this needless waste of lives
How many of you have gone so far,
as to curse and with a frown
Say for a driver's license,
they should have turned him down
Well let me tell you something,
about the kid behind the wheel
The habits he now practices he did not have to steal

Where did he get the idea
that it's smart to drive that way
He probably learned it from his "pop"
who drives the same today
But "pop" does not believe this,
he does not want to feel

That he is to blame for the actions
of the kid behind the wheel
Where did he learn to drink and drive,
perhaps it was from "pop"
When on a trip at several "joints,"
the "old boy" had to stop
To get a "brew" and talk a while,
then drive the roads like mad
Passing cars on hills and curves,
was this good for the lad

More and more I think of this,
the more it makes me feel
That "pop" is just as dangerous
as the kid behind the wheel
Just when will all the parents,
try to smarten up and see
For their kids to be safe drivers,
they themselves must be
Safe considerate drivers,
a good example for their son
And never will they be sorry
for something he has done
So let us set the right example,
they will live more happily
And live a longer life of fun,
and I grant you so will we

I wrote this poem for Sheriff Michael Neustrom of Lafayette Parish for the day he was sworn in. I used it as my introduction of him to those in attendance. He had it hanging on the wall in his office.

THE "SHERIFF'S BADGE"

Today we'll pin the "Sheriff's Badge"
on a sincere man
He'll say the words, "SO HELP ME GOD,"
he knows, he wants, he can
Trusting, good, a man of faith,
does describe him best
His deep desire to serve you well,
will surely meet the test
Fighting crime and the scourge of drugs,
is no simple task
But he will work to get it done,
there is no need to ask
Building trust and confidence,
in those who work for you
Will always be a goal for him,
in all the things they do
Always there to lend an ear, and try to understand
And when the need arises, extend a helping hand
With his staff, they'll do their best,
to "protect and serve"
Giving you that peace of mind, that you all deserve
Today we'll pin the "Sheriff's Badge"
on a humble man
With our prayers and trust in God,
he'll do the job...he can

I wrote this poem on November 11, 2010 when I was invited to address a group of World War II Veterans who were meeting at the Hilton in Lafayette.

THEN AND NOW

It's been many years, since World War Two
You did the job, you were asked to do
Our world was rocked by bomb and flame
You faced and stopped, the ones to blame
Against all odds, you fought and won
Not all came home, when it was done
Peace on earth was finally seen
You put an end to war's machine
Our flag flew high, that wall came down
Peace bells tolled in every town
On land and sea, and in the air
The joy of peace was everywhere
It's been many years, since World War Two
Yes, America is proud of you

Then nine-one-one, two thousand one
Clouds of smoke did hide the sun
Our country rocked by men from hell
Thousands died as buildings fell
Steel and glass, lay on the ground
With human carnage all around
Millions cried and we still mourn
For all of those, whose lives were torn
A giant emerged from all that dust
And we will do, the things we must
Yes, sneak attacks, upon our land
Will be avenged with heavy hand
Those evil men who did this deed
They will be found, we will succeed

I wrote this for a Police Memorial in 2012.

THE THIN BLUE LINE NEEDS JESUS

The thin blue line is thinner,
we lost some in our ranks
And yet we are much stronger,
for this we give Him thanks
We know that we must strengthen,
our just belief in Him
The times we feel outnumbered,
and odds look mighty slim
We need to call on Jesus, yes, He will show the way
The thin blue thin gets stronger,
when we take time to pray

The thin blue line's in mourning,
much sorrow for our loss
We know they are with Jesus,
who died upon that cross
They gave their lives believing,
in what they had to do
And we must keep their memory,
so dear to me and you
The thin blue line is thinner,
but God will lend a hand
The thin blue line has members,
in heaven's Angel band

The thin blue line gets stronger,
when God is on our side
And you and I are thankful,
when He comes for the ride
When he becomes our partner,
as we patrol our beats

72

We have no better back-up, in making safer streets
Our thin blue line is stronger,
our faith will see us through
A thin blue line no longer, our Father be with you

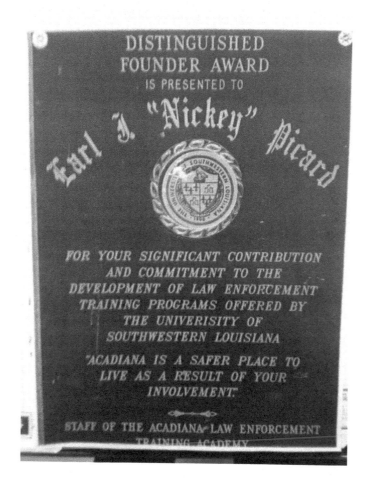

I wrote this poem for those who do not believe there
is a God.

THERE TRULY IS A HIM

Dear God, we pray for those
who don't believe in You
Some want You out of CHRISTmas,
they know not what they do
They took You out of schools,
and now some make demand
To rip You from the flag, that represents our land
"In God We Trust," "So Help Me God,"
they'd rather we not use
And Your great commandments
are merely don'ts and do's
How can a prayer be harmful,
how can a hymn be wrong
Just what is it they fear, when we honor You in song
How can they not be grateful,
after all that You have done
When for all the sins of man,
You gave Your only Son
With Your love and wisdom,
we now will pray for them
Perhaps they'll find this CHRISTmas,
there truly is a Him

This is one of the several poems I wrote for the
Police Memorial Program held in May of each year
for the Lafayette Police Department.

TO HONOR AND TO PRAY

Tonight we gather in this church
to honor and to pray
We honor those who gave their lives,
this is their special day
We pray that God will reassure
they did not die in vain
We pray that God will always be
with those who still remain
We pray that all will lend support
in the fight on crime
So men of greed no longer thrive
in this day and time

Tonight we gather in this church
and also pray for peace
We pray for peace throughout the world,
we pray for wars to cease
We know that God is fair and just,
and we must be the same
For when we do the work we do,
we do so in His name
Tonight we gather in this church
in honor and in prayer
We pray for God to be our Guide
and with us every where

This is one of several poems I wrote and presented at the 100 Club Banquet held each year at the Petroleum Club where local Police Officers were recognized and honored for work above and beyond their call of duty.

THIS JOB I DO

I pause a while give thanks to God
before I start my day
Then pin my badge and strap my gun,
I work my job this way
I thank my Lord for giving me,
a chance to serve mankind
And do the job that must be done
to give them peace of mind
I do this job for little pay, I do this out of choice
And while I see the things I see,
I must not raise my voice
I must not strike unless I'm struck
and then I best be right
For if I'm wrong or thought to be,
the noose will be drawn tight
Before I draw and use my gun,
I have to keep in mind
That if my case be brought to court,
my seat is in a bind

Now some have said that I am nuts,
my job they would not do
To them I say that might be so but this I do for you
In winter's cold and summer's heat,
throughout the night and day
To help to make this city safe for folks
to work and play

I see the bad, I see the good,
I see the wrong and right
I see the fears and see the joys,
share sorrow and delight
I thank the Lord, He prays for me
while keeping me from harm
From evil deeds of evil men and
from the weather's storm
I save my badge, secure my gun,
as I kneel down to pray
I spend some time and thank the Lord,
for giving me this day

This is one of the several poems I wrote for the
Police Memorial Program held in May of each year
for the Lafayette Police Department. This event was
on May 14, 2009.

TONIGHT WE HONOR HEROES

Tonight we honor heroes,
with love, respect and pride
Tonight we honor heroes, recalling why they died
We know they died believing,
in what they swore to do
Our heroes gave their lives, protecting me and you
We dedicate our prayers, to our heroes on this night
We promise to remember,
and keep their goals in sight

Tonight we honor heroes, and those they left behind
We pray that they find comfort,
and lasting peace of mind
We sadly feel their loss, we truly share their pain
We pray and trust they know, they did not die in vain
Tonight we honor heroes,
with love, respect and pride
They earned their place in heaven,
in God we can confide

This is one of the several poems I wrote for The Police Memorial Program held in May of each year for The Lafayette Police Department. This event was held on May 5, 2004.

WE OWE THEM TO REMEMBER

We owe them to remember, as we come to pray
Those who wore the badges, that we wear today
We owe them to remember, the sacrifice they made
We owe them to remember,
not let their memories fade
We owe them to remember, those they left behind
Pray that God keeps giving them
some peace of mind
We owe them to remember, we serve and we protect
For the laws that we enforce, we must have respect

We owe them to remember, the job we swore to do
We swore to serve all people, not just a chosen few
We owe them to remember,
to keep our standards high
Not do things to anyone, that we can't justify
We owe them to remember, as we protect and serve
We will give the people, the service they deserve
We owe them to remember, we pray to God tonight
To always give us courage, to always do what's right

I wrote this poem after a Louisiana State Trooper was shot and killed near Bell City, Louisiana and a Harris County Texas Deputy Sheriff was shot and killed in Houston, Texas while fueling up in his patrol car at a station.

WHEN A POLICE OFFICER IS SHOT AND KILLED

When a police officer is shot and killed
The precious blood of America has been spilled
A part of America needlessly dies
And a part of America openly cries
The heart of America also grieves
Yet the will of America never leaves
Because it's America we will survive
Their memories forever will be alive
Each night before you close your eyes
Say a prayer for those gals and guys
As you rest throughout the night
They're making sure that things are right

I wrote this poem to show my feelings for Lafayette
after being born and raised here and have no plans
to move and live in any other place.

WHY LAFAYETTE IS GREATEST

LAFAYETTE is greatest, there is no better place
For when the good Lord made it,
He showered it with grace
He took the finest people,
and scattered them around
It has become a fountain,
where hope and love abound
A lot of "Cajun flavor," He stirred into this pot
And that famous "joie de vive," is what it's all about

As we count our blessings, of much we can be proud
For we have been a model,
with voice so strong and loud
Friendly to our neighbors, we lend a helping hand
Yes, this is why God made us,
the "Hub of Cajun Land"
We are friendly people, our arms are open wide
We love to meet new people,
and show our "Cajun pride"

Sure, we have our problems,
but we will work them out
We'll overcome these bad times,
of this there is no doubt
LAFAYETTE is greatest, because our people are
The kind who work together, this they know us for
And I feel that we were blessed,
that God did not forget
To make this piece of heaven,
we know as LAFAYETTE!

This award was presented to Marshall Earl J. "Nickey" Picard by the Judges and Staff of the City Court of Lafayette in grateful appreciation of his many years of service as both Court Administrator and City Marshal.

POEM WRITTEN BY JUDGE DOUGLAS J. SALOOM

In everyone's life there comes a day
When a door must close and we walk away
For one of our own that day draws near
As he starts a new career, far, far, from here
It has been thirty plus years
since his right hand he did raise
But to him "So Help Me God"
was much more than a phrase
To Family, to Country and to Community
his time he has shared
Looking back it is easy to see how he fared
Medals, honors and plaques decorate his office walls
It saw briefings, meetings and yes to missing
defendant's late night calls
Near the bricks of this courtroom,
pictures of past Marshals do rest
But it is without question,
Earl J. "Nickey" Picard, well, he was the best

I wrote this because of all the ugly things going on in God's Great Country.

DARKNESS IS FALLING ON THE LIGHT OF THE WORLD

There are riots and destruction in the air
Soon there will be no more glare
GOD made this world and left it to us,
To keep it safe and free
We have made it much darker, can't everyone see
We have taken the beauty that GOD freely made
We have turned it to ugly and brought ugly shade
GOD is not happy for what we have done
Darkened the daylight, yes dampened HIS sun
HIS skies of blue, we have turned to gray
GOD is not pleased with this today
HE will come back to claim what is HIS
Not being pleased with the way that it is
All of HIS work is being torn down
We have given HIM reason for wearing a frown
HE trusted our thinking, HE trusted our care
But we have all faltered and don't seem to care
We need to turn eyes to Heaven
and beg for HIS trust
That we will restore it, THIS IS A MUST!

God blessed America and I'm sure that He's not happy about what we're doing to this great country.

GOD BLESSED AMERICA, HE DID FOR YOU AND ME

God made this great country, for the brave and free
HE made this country where dreams come true
Where we can do the things, we love to do
Its beauty is a wonder, throughout this entire land
It is free for everyone, if they lend a hand
There is no other country, to it we can compare
There is no other country, that has the love and care
So many freedoms we enjoy, no others can proclaim
In many other countries,
we can't use our Father's name
You never hear of Easter, Christmas has no season
There even is no mention of the reason
This is a God-made country,
HE made for you and me
Thank God for this great country,
HE made for the brave and free

Charles LaLanne was a longtime friend of mine. His daughter asked me to write a poem to be read at his Memorial Service on July 5, 2020.

HERE LIES A SOLDIER
TRUE TO THE NAME

Here lies a soldier true to the name
Yes, he was a soldier as true as one came
In defense of his country, in defense of his state
He stood ready to serve with honor and faith
Yes, Charles did stand ready in case of a call
Yes, Charles did stand ready to give it his all
No matter the duty no matter the time
He would show up and ready at the drop of a dime
His heart was all in it, body and soul
For he was a soldier on service patrol
He so loved his family, gave them his love
His faith was in Heaven and God up above
Here lies a soldier true to the name
Yes, he was a soldier true to the name
Yes, he was a soldier as true as one came
Now serving with Jesus in his Heavenly Band
He answered the call to God's Holy Land
His new station of duty is Heaven above
He will be guarding this place with all of his love

EARL J. "Nickey" PICARD

PERSONAL BACKGROUND:

◊ Born and reared in Lafayette, La.-October 10, 1931
◊ Educated in Lafayette public schools
◊ Married to Cecille Jeanette Dupuis Picard, April 3, 1949 - Nov. 19, 2019
◊ Father of three children: Leslie, Darlene and Timothy; two grandsons: Jake and Trevor (deputy sheriff in Iberia Parish)

RETIRED COMMAND SERGEANT MAJOR-LOUISIANA

◊ Army National Guard-1990
◊ Member of American Legion Post #69
◊ Speaks French and English
◊ 3RD and 4TH Degree Knight of Columbus

LAW ENFORCEMENT/CRIMINAL JUSTICE BACKGROUND

◊ 61 years of service, career began April 5, 1953 with Louisiana State Police
◊ Lafayette Parish Sheriff's Office-Chief Investigator-Assistant Chief Deputy
◊ Coordinator/Investigator Office of the District Attorney-Lafayette Parish
◊ Juvenile Detention Home Administrator
◊ Member of Louisiana Crime Commission
◊ First Lafayette City Court Administrator
◊ June 1ST, 1984 became 10TH Marshal in Lafayette history; first to be elected to five consecutive 6-year terms upon his re-election in 2008.

LAW ENFORCEMENT AND RELATED SCHOOLS/TRAINING

◊ Louisiana State Police Training Academy-1953
◊ LSU In-Service Training Basic and Advanced
◊ LSU In-Service Training Homicide Investigation
◊ Southern Police Institute-University of Louisville-Louisville, Kentucky-1960
◊ Federal Bureau of Narcotics-Washington, DC 1964
◊ University of Southwestern Louisiana
◊ University of Houston, Houston, Texas
◊ Penn State University, University Park, PA
◊ National Center for State Courts, Denver, CO
◊ National Center for State Courts, Minneapolis, MN
◊ National District Attorney's Association
◊ Conferences on Narcotics And Juvenile Justice
◊ International Symposium on Drunk Driving,
◊ Washington. DC

INSTRUCTOR:

LSU In-Service Training Program
Acadiana Law Enforcement Training Academy and
Area Reserve Police Training Academies

AWARDS:

◊ Recognition award presented by Louisiana Director of Public Safety for work in traffic safety field-1954 for poems "The Kid Behind the Wheel" and "Did You?"
◊ Lafayette Area "Lawman of The Year" - 1970

◊ Kiwanis International "Lawman of The Year" Louisiana-Mississippi-West Tennessee District-1970
◊ Founders Award - Acadiana Law Enforcement Training Academy (ALETA)
◊ Past President Louisiana City Marshals
◊ Past President Louisiana National Guard Enlisted
◊ Association
◊ Army Commendation Medal
◊ Army Achievement Medal
◊ Louisiana Commendation Medal
◊ Louisiana "Senior Non-Commission Officer of The
◊ Year" 1982
◊ Sons of the American Revolution "Law Enforcement Award"
◊ Inducted into Louisiana Justice Hall of Fame 2005
◊ Recognized by Lafayette Optimist Club for "Respect for Law and Service"
◊ Honored "Lawman of the Year" St. Jude Council Knights of Columbus 2005
◊ Recognized by Louisiana State Legislature for 55 Years of Service 2008
◊ Recognized by Louisiana Attorney General for 55 Years of Service 2008
◊ Marshal's Office awarded "Recognition Award" 2007
◊ and 2010 and awarded "Accreditation Award in 2013" by the Commission on Accreditation for Law Enforcement Agencies (CALEA) and is the only Marshal's office in Louisiana and only agency of its type in the nation to be so honored.

◊ Inducted as "Living Legend" into Acadian Museum 2009
◊ Recognized by the Lafayette Consolidated Council as "Outstanding Citizen" 2009
◊ "2009 Lawman of the Year" St. EDMOND KNIGHTS of Columbus Council
◊ Elected Trustee Municipal Employees Retirement System (MERS) 2011
◊ Elected At-Large Member Parish Democratic Executive Committee-2012
◊ DPEC Lifetime Achievement Award-Hall of Fame 2014
◊ State Police Superintendent Award of Excellence 2014 (first award of this type presented)
◊ Retired as Lafayette City Marshal on December 31, 2014 after serving 30 years and 7 months as Marshal
◊ 2015 Lafayette League of Women's Voters-Safeguarding Democracy Award

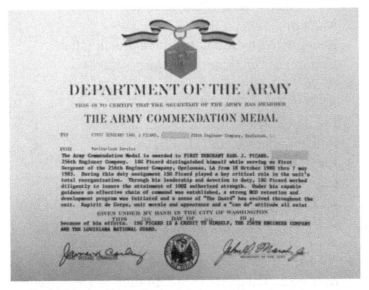

Military career medals

Sgt Major, 1983

Awarded for Senior
Non-Commissioned
Officer of Louisiana,
in 1982

Graduation photo at
University of Louisville,
Kentucky in Police Science
& Administration, 1961

Lafayette, Louisiana
Kiwanis Club, Lawman
of the Year, 1970

Recognition
Certificate of
Appreciation
by the
Louisiana
State Police
for his poems
"DID YOU?"
and "THE
KID BEHIND
THE
WHEEL";
1956

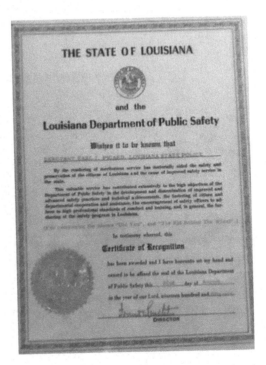

"In everyone's life there comes a day;
When a door must close and we walk away;
For one of our own that day draws near;
As he starts a new chapter far, far from here;
It has been thirty plus years since his right hand he did raise;
But to him "So Help Me God" was much more than a phrase;
To Family, to Country and to Community his time he has shared;
Looking back it is easy to see how he fared;
Medals, honors and plaques decorate his office walls;
It saw briefings, meetings and yes to missing defendants late night calls;
Near the bricks of this courtroom, pictures of past Marshals do rest;
But it is without question, Earl J. "Nickey" Picard, well, he was the best!"

Presented to Marshal Earl J. "Nickey" Picard by the Judges and Staff
of the City Court of Lafayette in grateful appreciation of his many years
of service to the Court, both Court Administrator and City Marshal.
Poem written by Judge Douglas J. Saloom

Poem written by Judge Douglas Saloom and
presented on December 14, 2014.

PROCLAMATION

WHEREAS, Earl J. Picard was born in Lafayette, Louisiana on October 10, 1931. His parents were the late Henry Avery Picard and the late Levee Marie Durio; and

WHEREAS, Earl was one of six boys and had only one sister. He was affectionately given the nickname "Nickey." Having been raised in Lafayette, he received his education in Lafayette Parish schools and learned to speak French; and

WHEREAS, on April 3, 1949, he married Cecille Jeanette Dupuis at Saint Genevieve Catholic Church. They had three children: two sons, Leslie and Timothy and daughter, Darlene; and

WHEREAS, Earl began his law enforcement career in April 1953. His work history includes the Louisiana State Police, the Lafayette Parish Sheriff's Office, the Investigator Office of the District Attorney, the Juvenile Detention Home, and the First Administrator of City Court of Lafayette on September 1, 1980; and

WHEREAS, appointed on June 1, 1984, his work as Marshal of the City Court of Lafayette is to be commended. As the tenth Marshal in its history, Marshal Picard brought Lafayette City Marshal's Office into the 21st century and many felt his was the premier Marshal's Office in the State of Louisiana. Having served for 30 years and 7 months, he has made history as the longest-serving Marshal in the history of the Court.

NOW, THEREFORE, I, Josh Guillory, Mayor-President, in coordination with Lafayette City Councilman Patrick Lewis and Lafayette Parish Councilman John J. Guilbeau of the Lafayette Council, are proud to bestow upon Earl J. "Nickey" Picard the title of

"HONORARY LIFETIME LAFAYETTE CITY MARSHAL"

IN WITNESS WHEREOF, we have hereunto set our hands and caused the Seal of the Lafayette Consolidated Government to be affixed this 4th day of February 2020.

_____
PATRICK LEWIS, CHAIR
LAFAYETTE CITY COUNCIL, DISTRICT 1

_____
JOHN J. GUILBEAU, VICE-CHAIR
LAFAYETTE PARISH COUNCIL, DISTRICT 4

_____
JOSH GUILLORY, MAYOR-PRESIDENT
LAFAYETTE CONSOLIDATED GOVERNMENT

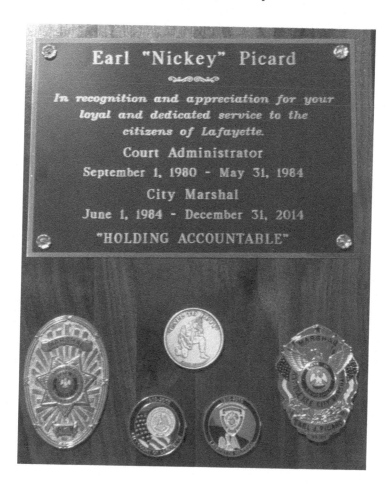

For USA and non-USA buyers, get this book from Amazon.com.

Questions or comments? Contact the publisher at (888) 606-3257.

www.CypressCovePublishing.com